22 WALKS AROUND GLEN

Walks are all graded in difficulty, terrain
ability to enable them to select walks wit

G000093537

Weather could change quickly so it is important to have appropriate clothing and
equipment for the walk. Boots, water/windproof, warm clothing, hat and gloves are
recommended. A day sack with food, emergency items and spare clothing should
be carried.

Two maps can be used with this book, which are **O.S. Explorer No. 392. Ben
Nevis & Fort William** (recommended), or **O.S Landranger No. 41. Ben Nevis, Fort
William & Glen Coe**. It is also recommended a compass and/or GPS be carried for
use in bad weather conditions.

ACKNOWLEDGEMENTS
Clothing & Equipment - Berghaus "Extrem" Range (Front Cover)
Graphic Design - Jamie Mann.

First Published 2014
ISBN 978-1-903568-71-2
Challenge Publications, 7, Earlsmere Drive, Barnsley S71 5HH
www.chall-pub.co.uk or **www.national3peaks.co.uk**

Start/Parking: Braveheart car park, on the right, which is the first after entering the Glen 1.3km from Nevis Bridge GR.122737

Terrain: Easy walk on a track and path with only a short ascent.

Comment: This walk can incorporate a visit to Glen Nevis Visitor Centre. There are good views of the Ben path leading up from the Visitor Centre and of the Glen itself.

1. From Braveheart car park, descend the short distance to the main road then turn right walking for 1km on the footpath to a sign on your right pointing to The West Highland Way along a short path between fields. Before you arrive there you pass a large wishing stone at the side of the footpath, which has a plaque near it.

2. You then pass the entrance to Glen Nevis Visitor Centre on your left before you reach The West Highland Way sign on your right.

3. Turn onto the West Highland Way path walking for 120m to a kissing gate, which you go through to ascend a short distance to a wide forest track running left to right.

4. Turn right at this point. A sign points left to The West Highland Way but you turn right.

5. Keep on the wide track through the forest on a general bearing of 18°M for 1.1km, which leads back to Braveheart car park where you originally started.

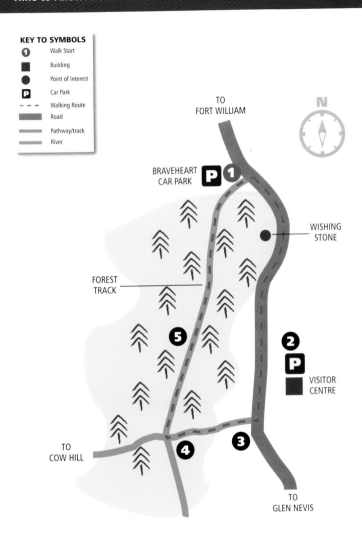

KEY TO SYMBOLS

❶	Walk Start
■	Building
●	Point of Interest
🅿	Car Park
– – –	Walking Route
	Road
	Pathway/track
	River

TO
FORT WILLIAM

N

BRAVEHEART
CAR PARK 🅿 ❶

WISHING
STONE

FOREST
TRACK

❺

❷
🅿

VISITOR
CENTRE

TO
COW HILL

❹

❸

TO
GLEN NEVIS

NOT TO SCALE

Start: At the ferry landing of the Camusnagaul Ferry beside the fish restaurant on the dual carriageway skirting Fort William.
Telephone for ferry times: 07813 558364
Price in 2014 £2.00 each way (adult).

Terrain: Single track road then heather fern/grass path to summit. Stony path descending back to the road again.

Comment: A nice walk with an ascent, steep in parts but achievable and not too long. Magnificent views from the top. Safe for the family, requiring care at the top.

1. Leaving the ferry, turn right on the road where you will soon cross a cattle grid. Walk around a left hand bend then just after, look for a marker post on your left and worn path ascending through the trees and bracken. Look for the marker posts as you ascend to a deer fence.

2. Look for the gate in the fence, go through and walk for about 30m then turn right to ascend a feint path to the mast on the top. The path disappears but keep ascending and look up the hillside for a telegraph pole. On reaching it, continue walking nearby a further line of poles directly to the mast on the hillside.

3. There are views across to Fort William and Ben Nevis beyond. To the right are Lock Linnhe and the exit towards the isles. To the left are Caol, Corpach, the Caledonian Canal and Great Glen.

4. Should you wish to walk a further 2km each way, look up the mountain to the summit of Meall an t-Slamain and look for the ascending path. If you cannot see the path, walk between the bracken to the summit. It is quite visible and straightforward. Once there, return to the mast which you should see, and pick up the obvious access track from the mast leading to the road.

5. The winding track takes you down to the deer fence. Go through the gate or cross stile there and continue down the service track to the road. At the road, turn right, walking for 3km along the road and back over the cattle grid to the ferry landing.

Ferry to mast return 2.7 km. (1.68 miles)
Ferry to summit return 6.7km (4.16 miles)

Rating: MODERATE
Time: 2 hours 30 minutes*

*To the mountain summit, add a further 1 hour 15 minutes.

6. There is a tea room 400m along the road, but it is only open Wednesday to Saturday. Ensure you do not miss the last ferry (4.35pm) - Confirm time on your outward journey, as it is a long walk all the way around back to Fort William!

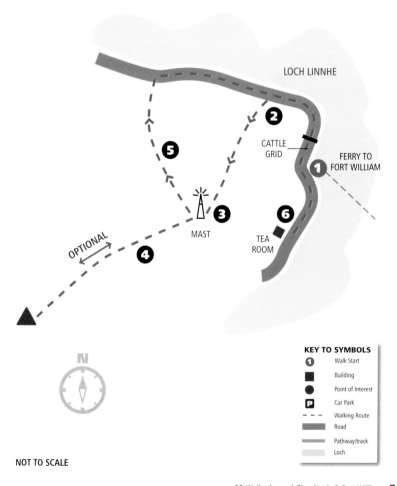

NOT TO SCALE

Walk 3 - Loch Linnhe View Walk

Start/Parking: Beside the picnic area at the top of Lundavra Road on the road to Blarmachfoldach. GR. NN096721

Terrain: Grass and narrow track to the summit

Comment: An easy walk with a reasonably easy ascent (if you take it steady) to the summit giving excellent views along Loch Linnhe and to the mountains opposite. A good walk to take children on to tire them out and not too long!

1. Leaving the picnic area access gate, cross the road and go through the farm gate opposite into the field. Ascend the field and head for a farm gate well ahead up the field with a small kissing gate next to it.

2. Go through the gate and keep on the path ascending to the top where the ground levels out more. The actual path continues a further 200m to the highest point of land and the 'trig' point there at 288m, but this is not evident until you get near the summit.

3. At the summit there are fine views to be had in all directions, particularly looking west along the loch towards the sea and islands. After taking in the magnificent views, return by the same route and descend to the picnic area beside the road lower down.

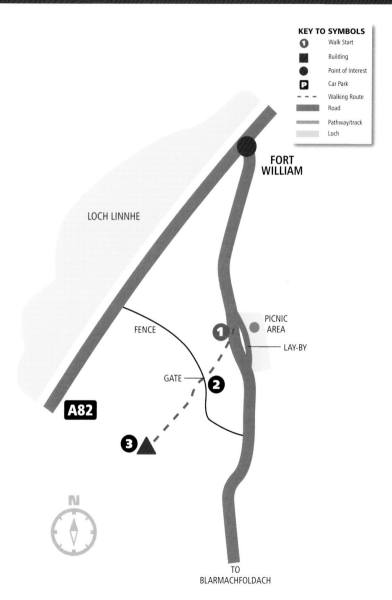

KEY TO SYMBOLS

- ① Walk Start
- ■ Building
- ● Point of Interest
- 🅿 Car Park
- - - - Walking Route
- Road
- Pathway/track
- Loch

FORT
WILLIAM

LOCH LINNHE

FENCE

① ·· PICNIC
AREA

LAY-BY

GATE ②

A82

③ ▲

N

TO
BLARMACHFOLDACH

NOT TO SCALE

Start/Parking: Glen Nevis Visitor Centre GR.123730

Terrain: Flat path, easy to follow.

Comment: A nice relaxing walk along the riverbank with clear water in the River Nevis flowing swiftly to the sea. The kids will enjoy this walk.

1. After parking at the Visitor Centre car park, pick up the path along by the river nearby. Walk on this path away from the Visitor Centre towards Fort William in a northerly direction to the suspension bridge 140m along the riverbank.

2. Cross the bridge following the sign to 'Ben path'. Continue on this path along the riverbank passing Achintee Farm (B&B) on your left. You can see the Visitor Centre on the opposite side of the river.

3. At a turning left for the Ben path, carry straight on along by the river do not take the path off to the left. You should now see the Glen Nevis Camping Park on the opposite side of the river as you progress on this flat path.

4. Cross four burns running into the river before coming to a footbridge spanning the River Nevis.

5. Cross this bridge where you should see the Glen Nevis Youth Hostel opposite.

6. Turn right crossing the road with care onto the footpath and walking for 1.4km, passing the camping park and a white house then an entrance to The West Highland Way on the left before crossing the road and going through an entrance into the Glen Nevis Visitor Centre again.

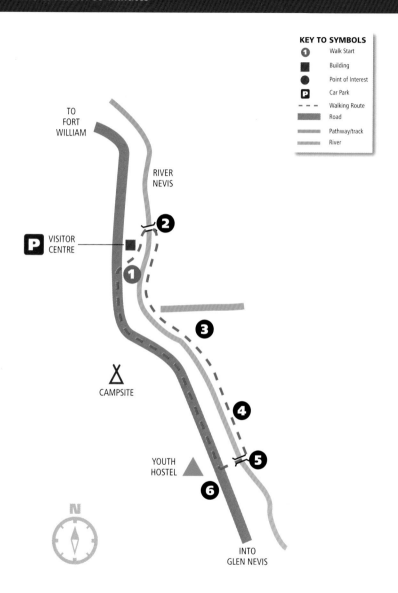

KEY TO SYMBOLS

1   Walk Start

■   Building

●   Point of Interest

P   Car Park

- - -   Walking Route

Road

Pathway/track

River

TO
FORT
WILLIAM

RIVER
NEVIS

P VISITOR
CENTRE

CAMPSITE

YOUTH
HOSTEL

INTO
GLEN NEVIS

N

NOT TO SCALE

Walk 5 - Nevis Forest Walk (circular)

Start/Parking: Glen Nevis Visitor Centre GR.123730

Terrain: Easy walk on a good path with a short ascent.

Comment: A pleasant walk with good views of Glen Nevis

1. Leave the Visitor Centre by turning left along the Glen Nevis road into the Glen then walk for 1.1km to the Glen Nevis Restaurant on the opposite side of the road.

2. Turn right there where a small sign for The West Highland Way points along the metalled road.

3. Walk between the houses at the far end of the road and bear left onto a stony path near a small garage.

4. Walk through a kissing gate beside a 5-bar gate leading into the forest, where a sign on the gate states 'walkers welcome here'. Ascend for a short distance to a wider track running left to right.

5. Turn right here then soon after a path joins from the left, but continue straight ahead for 700m to a waymark sign.

6. Turn right, down to a kissing gate then onto the main road 120m further on.

7. Turn left at the road then right soon after, through a narrow opening taking you back into Glen Nevis Visitor Centre.

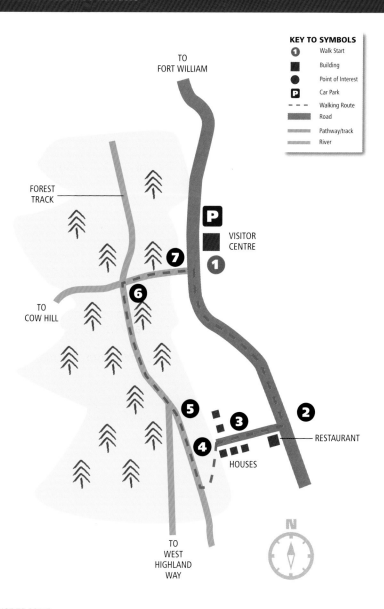

TO
FORT WILLIAM

KEY TO SYMBOLS

- ① Walk Start
- ■ Building
- ● Point of Interest
- P Car Park
- - - - Walking Route
- Road
- Pathway/track
- River

FOREST
TRACK

P

VISITOR
CENTRE

⑦

①

TO
COW HILL

⑥

⑤

③

②

④

RESTAURANT

HOUSES

TO
WEST
HIGHLAND
WAY

N

NOT TO SCALE

Walk 6 - Water of Nevis Walk (circular)

Start/Parking: At the bridge over the River Nevis at Achriabhach in Glen Nevis GR.145684. Park in the car park just before the two bridges or just over the bridges.

Terrain: Narrow but safe grass, small stone and hard path up the glen with a descending road to the bridge. Not too steep and suitable for most of the family with only short ascents.

Comment: All the family will like this one. It is not too long, safe and enjoyable with good viewing all round.

1. Leaving the car park just before the two bridges, walk down and go through a small gate on your right, just by the river. Keep the river on the left side as you continue on a narrow path close by it. The walk starts on a flat path but after 900m, it starts to ascend gradually.

2. You pass through a wooded area on the narrow path and continue ascending. Ahead, on your left you may see a water slide descending from Carn Dearg, which looks spectacular, especially after rainfall.

3. Continue on the path as it undulates over the hillside. You come to a footbridge over the Waters of Nevis further up the glen on the left side. Cross the bridge to emerge on the single-track minor road.

4. Turn left to walk down the minor road with care back to the bridge where you started.

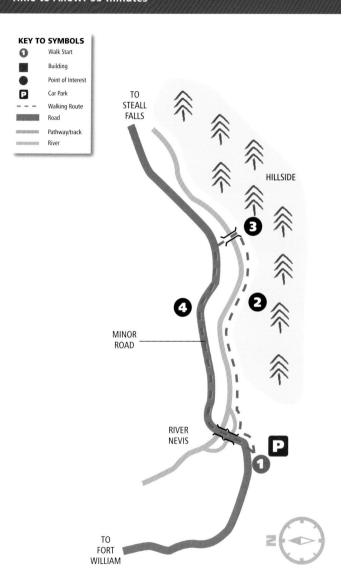

KEY TO SYMBOLS

- ❶ Walk Start
- ■ Building
- ● Point of Interest
- 🅿 Car Park
- - - - Walking Route
- ▬ Road
- ▬ Pathway/track
- ▬ River

TO
STEALL
FALLS

HILLSIDE

❸

❹

❷

MINOR
ROAD

RIVER
NEVIS

🅿

❶

TO
FORT
WILLIAM

NOT TO SCALE

Start: Glen Nevis Visitor Centre GR.123730

Parking: Glen Nevis Visitor Centre

Terrain: Footpath, road and stony path. Short, slight ascent/descent.

Comment: A good introduction to Glen Nevis and the outstanding scenery of the area, easy.

1. After parking your car, walk to the Glen Nevis road and turn right. Continue on the footpath towards Fort William and 150m before the roundabout at the entrance to the Glen, look for a small bridge on your right, crossing the River Nevis.

2. Cross the old bridge and turn right at the far side. Continue on the road and when you get to a shop on the right side after 300m, keep right and continue round the outside of the estate. The road turns to a single-track road as you pass the sports field. The River Nevis is just off to your right as you walk.

3. Continue for 2km to a parking area beside the Ben Nevis Inn. Inside there is a picture window where you can overlook the foothills of Ben Nevis and watch the tired walkers returning from 'the Ben'. Food is also available here.

4. Leaving the Ben Nevis Inn, turn right through a farm gate and along a stony path. Look for a step stile on your right and cross to descend a long straight path towards the river at the bottom. At the bottom corner of the path, turn right and walk along to the footbridge over the river.

5   Crossing the bridge you emerge in the car park of the Visitor Centre in Glen Nevis where you started.

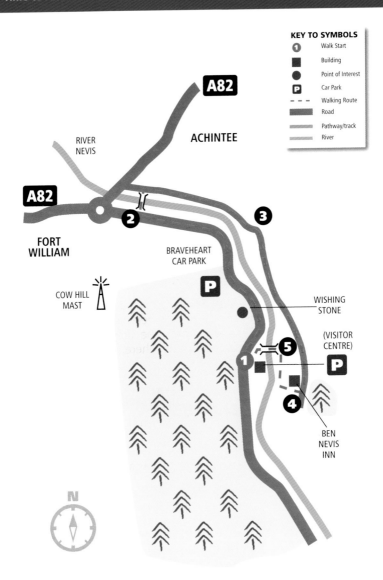

KEY TO SYMBOLS

- ➊ Walk Start
- ■ Building
- ● Point of Interest
- 𝐏 Car Park
- – – – Walking Route
- Road
- Pathway/track
- River

A82

RIVER
NEVIS

ACHINTEE

A82

**FORT
WILLIAM**

COW HILL
MAST

BRAVEHEART
CAR PARK

WISHING
STONE

(VISITOR
CENTRE)

BEN
NEVIS
INN

N

NOT TO SCALE

Start/Parking: Annat Industrial Estate. GR. NN078770

Terrain: wide track then narrow track/grass path, feint in places but obvious route.

Comment: An easy walk ascending the right of the waterfalls then descending the left side some distance away.

1. After parking, walk to the main road; turn right, walking for 150m to a sign pointing left to Annat. Turn left there and ascend a single track road for approx. 300m. Cross the bridge on the right then turn left onto a stony access track and ascend for 1km, passing waterfalls behind the trees on your left. Pass a small water pumping station before the track comes to an end.

2. To your right is a deer fence and gate leading into woodland, straight ahead is a narrow path bearing left. Take the path ahead and follow it round bearing left and becoming narrower. Cross a small footbridge then another and stay on the undulating narrow path. It leads onto open moorland towards a mast which is now ahead.

3. On your left in the glen is Corpach and a large factory near where you started. Follow the winding path gradually bearing left to an opening in the fence. Go through and proceed on the feint path down the moor. Stay on the path with the stream and waterfalls well off to your left and as you descend you can see the track you ascended on your far left.

4. Your path gradually winds round in a semi-circle to the waterfall near the bottom. The path joins a wider stony track near the bottom end, and as you descend it becomes wider. You can hear the noise of the stream on your left now.

5. Go through a metal 5-bar gate and after 50m you are back on the road you started from. Turn right and descend the road and join the main road at the bottom. At the main road, turn right and walk for 150m back to Annat Industrial Estate where you parked your vehicle.

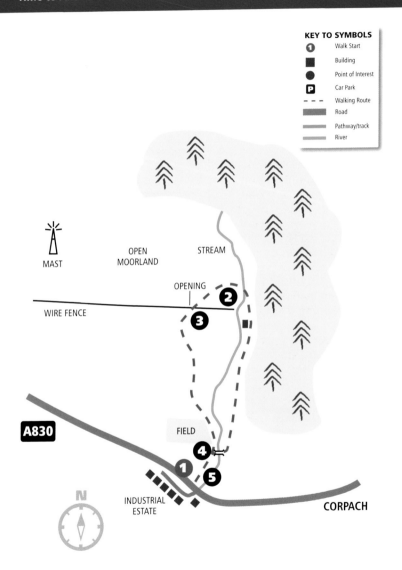

KEY TO SYMBOLS

❶	Walk Start
■	Building
●	Point of Interest
🅿	Car Park
- - -	Walking Route
	Road
	Pathway/track
	River

MAST

OPEN MOORLAND

STREAM

OPENING

WIRE FENCE

❷

❸

A830

FIELD

❹

❶ ❺

INDUSTRIAL ESTATE

CORPACH

N

NOT TO SCALE

Walk 9 - Ben Path Walk (circular)

Start/Parking: Glen Nevis Visitor Centre GR.123730

Terrain: Easy walk on a good path with a short ascent.

Comment: A good walk with excellent views along the Glen.

1. Leaving the Glen Nevis Visitor Centre entrance, walk on the path along by the river in a northerly direction to the suspension bridge nearby.

2. Cross the bridge following the 'Ben Path' sign. Continue on the obvious path for 360m, passing Achintee Farm (B&B) on your left. The Visitor Centre is now on the opposite side of the river.

3. You come to a left turn and another sign pointing to 'Ben Path' Follow this, walking up a straight path for 250m to some steps over a stone wall.

4. Climb over the wall steps then cross a farm track ascending on a stony path bearing right towards Ben Nevis. You have good views along the Glen in both directions.

5. You ascend gradually for 900m then join another path rising steeply from the right. Turn right here and descend to the bridge over the river and the youth hostel on the far side, which you should see below.

6. Descending to the youth hostel below, take care on the steep path. Just before crossing the River Nevis is an information board giving weather conditions on Ben Nevis.

7. Cross the bridge to the youth hostel then turn right, taking care in crossing, then walk for 1.4km back to Glen Nevis Visitor Centre. Pass the entrance to the camping park on your left then a white house (B&B) then an entrance to The West Highland Way on the left.

8. Cross the road again here towards the river and go through into the Visitor Centre car park again.

Distance: 5.2 km (3.23 miles)
Time to Allow: 1 hour 30 minutes

Rating: MODERATE

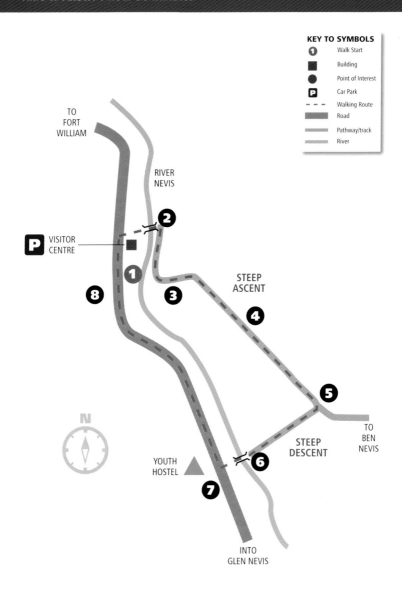

KEY TO SYMBOLS

1	Walk Start
■	Building
●	Point of Interest
P	Car Park
– – –	Walking Route
	Road
	Pathway/track
	River

TO
FORT
WILLIAM

RIVER
NEVIS

P VISITOR
CENTRE

STEEP
ASCENT

TO
BEN
NEVIS

STEEP
DESCENT

YOUTH
HOSTEL

INTO
GLEN NEVIS

N

NOT TO SCALE

Start/Parking: Glen Nevis Visitor Centre GR.123730

Terrain: Very steep ascent and descent for 750m on a well-defined path.

Comment: This is one of the harder walks but well worth the effort. Ensure you have some spare warm clothing to put on at the summit.

1. Turn left out of the Visitor Centre car park, cross with care, walk for 230m to an entrance leading to The West Highland Way.

2. Turn right here, a small sign denotes the route along a straight path between fields for 120m, to a kissing gate at the entrance to Nevis Forest.

3. Walk up the short path to meet a wider track, which you cross over then start ascending steeply up some steps that have a handrail at the side.

4. Continue on this steep ascent on a well-defined path through the forest to a kissing gate on higher ground, then on to a green post, which marks a turning off to the right leading to Cow Hill mast.

5. Turn right at the green post keeping on the stony path for 1.4km, crossing a stile then continuing on the undulating track leading to the mast, which you may see ahead, at GR.113735, cloud permitting.

6. When you reach the mast, take care in low cloud, and do not venture too far away from the mast itself. Good views of Fort William and the surrounding area abound from here.

7. Return on the same route to the Visitor Centre remembering to turn left at the green post and taking extra care on the descent.

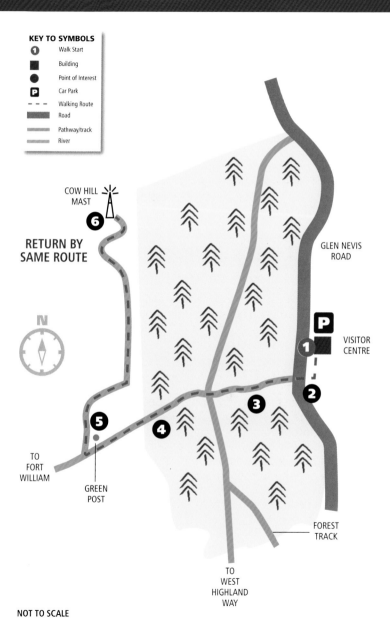

KEY TO SYMBOLS

- ① Walk Start
- ■ Building
- ● Point of Interest
- 🅿 Car Park
- - - - Walking Route
- Road
- Pathway/track
- River

COW HILL
MAST

⑥

**RETURN BY
SAME ROUTE**

Ⓝ

GLEN NEVIS
ROAD

🅿

① VISITOR
CENTRE

②

③

⑤

④

TO
FORT
WILLIAM

GREEN
POST

FOREST
TRACK

TO
WEST
HIGHLAND
WAY

NOT TO SCALE

Start/Parking: Glen Nevis Visitor Centre GR.123730

Terrain: Small stone path for most of the hillside route then footpath on entering Fort William back to the Visitor Centre. A gentle ascent and descent in the first half then flat for the return.

Comment: A nice easy walk with good views as you walk around the hillside.

1. Leaving Glen Nevis Visitor Centre car park, cross the road and turn right, walking towards the roundabout at the entrance to the glen. Walk for 200m to an opening on your left then walk a further 150m to a small stone path on your left leading between the bushes and trees.

2. Follow the path, which starts fairly flat and soon crosses a small footbridge. You emerge in Braveheart car park where you turn left on the road into it and walk to the signpost at the top of the car park. Turn right onto a stone path following the sign for town centre 2.5km.

3. The path soon starts to ascend as it skirts around the hillside. You come to a waymarker post, which states 'leisure centre ahead' and Peat Track to the left. Turn left on the Peat Track, where there are good views all along here of Fort William and Glen Nevis.

4. You come to another fork in the path where a sign points to Henderson Row ahead and the Peat Track is to your left. Walk ahead and you come to a small reservoir where you continue as the path starts to descend by a line of trees and then between the houses into Fort William.

5. Descending through Pinegrove cul de sac then Hill Road, you emerge by the park area and Tesco. Turn right and walk diagonally across the park beside Tesco to the main A82 road and continue in the same direction, passing the hospital and along to Nevis Bridge.

6. Follow the road and sign into Glen Nevis, and walk on the footpath back to the Visitor Centre, passing the wishing stone by the roadside on the way.

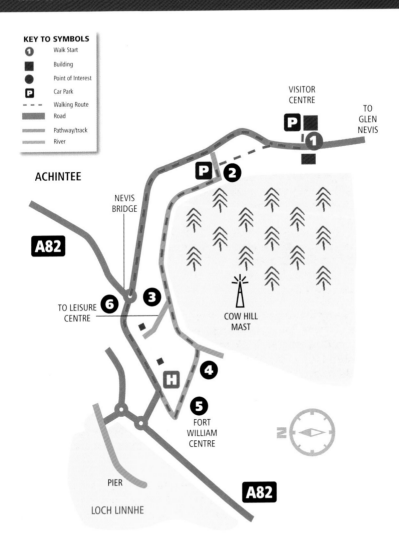

KEY TO SYMBOLS

❶	Walk Start
■	Building
●	Point of Interest
🅿	Car Park
- - -	Walking Route
▬	Road
▬	Pathway/track
▬	River

ACHINTEE

VISITOR CENTRE

TO GLEN NEVIS

NEVIS BRIDGE

A82

TO LEISURE CENTRE

COW HILL MAST

FORT WILLIAM CENTRE

H

PIER

LOCH LINNHE

A82

NOT TO SCALE

Start/Parking: Lower Falls car park GR.145683 (Lock valuables in car boot).

Terrain: Single track road then grass/stone path, can be slippery when wet.

Comment: A pleasant walk with good views of the river and a waterslide. The walk culminates in the spectacular Steall Falls waterfall in this hanging valley. This walk is not to be missed.

Note: Every year there are accidents involving people falling off the path that leads through Steall Gorge from the top car park in Glen Nevis. These can be fatal. Stay on the path at all times and wear proper footwear as slippery conditions can often be encountered on this path.

1. The Lower Falls car park is 200m past Achriabhach at the end of Nevis Forest.

2. Turn right out of the car park following the road over two small bridges with impressive waterfalls below. Stay on the road as you ascend for 2.4km to the Upper Falls car park where the road stops. Just before the car park you pass a water slide cascading down the mountainside on your left.

3. The footpath to Steall Falls starts here. The path can be very slippery when wet as it often is. Initially the path is stony and rutted but well defined as you walk parallel with the river below in the Glen.

4. The path crosses two small waterfalls coming down the mountainside on your left. It may be difficult walking over the wet stones for part of the route here.

5. Cross another waterfall, where looking down into the Glen you can see the river racing over the rocks on its journey down the Glen. Take care on the path, as there is a steep drop off to your right.

6. You come to a high point on the path then you descend to a wooden platform before ascending over it. Hold the handrail as you pass.

7. Rounding a bend in the path you see a spectacular waterfall dropping into the river at the far end of this hanging valley.

8. At the far side of this valley on the opposite side of the river is a mountain rescue hut/bothy. A rope bridge gives access to it. You have good views of Ben Nevis from here as you perhaps stop for a picnic before retracing your steps back to the car park.

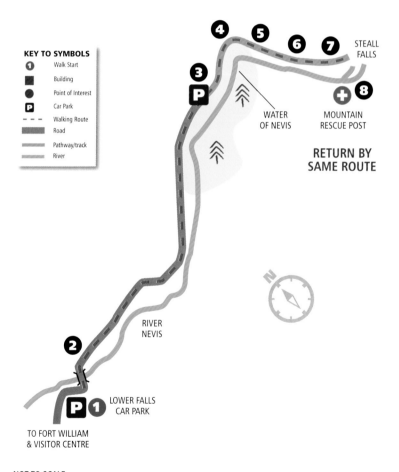

KEY TO SYMBOLS

❶	Walk Start
■	Building
●	Point of Interest
🅿	Car Park
– – –	Walking Route
▬	Road
▬	Pathway/track
▬	River

STEALL FALLS

WATER OF NEVIS

MOUNTAIN RESCUE POST

RETURN BY SAME ROUTE

RIVER NEVIS

LOWER FALLS CAR PARK

TO FORT WILLIAM & VISITOR CENTRE

NOT TO SCALE

Start: Opposite Glen Nevis Youth Hostel GR.128717

Parking: Lay-by near Glen Nevis Youth Hostel

Terrain: Very steep with a lot of loose stone on the path. Two steps forward and one back.

Comment: Very strenuous but worth the effort. Ensure you have suitable clothing and footwear for this walk.

1. Walk to the footbridge crossing the River Nevis opposite the youth hostel, cross the bridge then cross a fence with steps over it. An information board displays the current weather conditions on Ben Nevis.

2. Continue on the path, which now starts to ascend steeply as it twists around the mountainside. You join a path from the left on higher ground, but you keep right, still ascending the main Ben Nevis path.

3. You pass a seat on your ascent, then go over two small metal bridges on this extremely stony route. The path ascends along the side of Red Burn where you can hear the noise of the water rushing down the mountainside.

4. Just before reaching the loch, you see a conservation sign as you are ascending steeply.

5. Reaching the loch and hanging valley, the path levels out but around it is often very wet with natural springs. The area is exposed and can be inhospitable in bad weather but is an enjoyable picnic stop in good conditions.

6. Stay on the path to a sharp right hand bend then bear left towards the loch. There are numerous large stones to sit on, where there are good views in all directions.

7. You should return by the same route to the youth hostel.

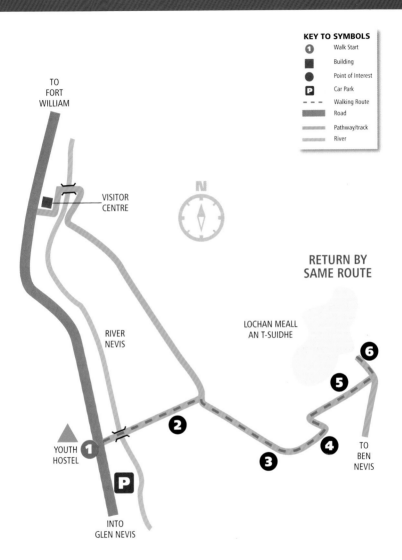

KEY TO SYMBOLS

1   Walk Start

  Building

  Point of Interest

P   Car Park

- - -   Walking Route

  Road

  Pathway/track

  River

TO
FORT
WILLIAM

VISITOR
CENTRE

N

RETURN BY
SAME ROUTE

RIVER
NEVIS

LOCHAN MEALL
AN T-SUIDHE

6

5

2

3

4

TO
BEN
NEVIS

YOUTH
HOSTEL

1

P

INTO
GLEN NEVIS

NOT TO SCALE

Start/Parking: Glen Nevis Visitors Centre GR.123730

Terrain: A steep ascent from the youth hostel, then undulating stony track followed by single-track road and forest track.

Comment: A pleasant walk in varying surroundings.

1. Leaving the Visitor Centre car park, turn left walking along the footpath for 1.4km to the youth hostel.

2. Cross the bridge opposite the youth hostel then turn left over some steps to an information board showing weather conditions on Ben Nevis.

3. Ascend steeply on a path, which winds around the hillside until you join another path from your left, coming from the Visitor Centre.

4. Turn left here and descend a stony path to a farm track beside a stone wall. Head for the Ben Nevis Inn and a small wood 200m further ahead where there is a car parking area next to it.

5. Continue on the undulating single-track road for 2km, passing houses and an electricity sub station. You come to a junction with a sign pointing to Achintee path.

6. Look on your left near the junction for the small footbridge across the River Nevis. Cross this then turn left on the Glen Nevis road, walking on the footpath to Braveheart car park on your right at the entrance to the forest.

7. Follow the sign for forest walk, going through the entrance to the top side of the car park onto a wide track into the forest and turn left. Continue for 1.2km to a path turning left near a waymark sign.

8. Turn left here descending to a kissing gate then along a path for 120m to the main road again.

9. Turn left at the main road, walking for 100m to the entrance into the Visitor Centre on the opposite side of the road.

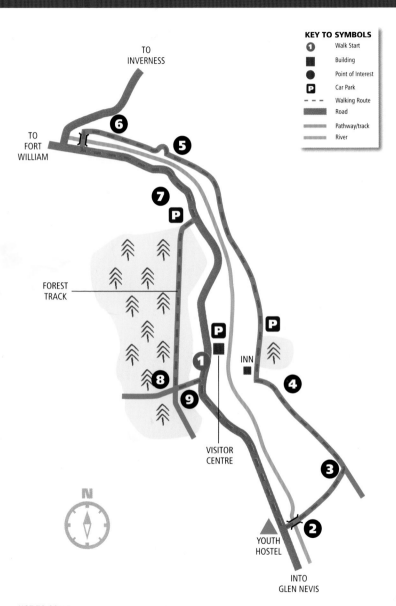

KEY TO SYMBOLS

- ① Walk Start
- ■ Building
- ● Point of Interest
- 🅿 Car Park
- - - - Walking Route
- ▬ Road
- ▬ Pathway/track
- ▬ River

TO INVERNESS

TO FORT WILLIAM

FOREST TRACK

INN

VISITOR CENTRE

YOUTH HOSTEL

INTO GLEN NEVIS

N

NOT TO SCALE

Walk 15 - Dun Deardail Fort (circular)

Start/Parking: Glen Nevis Visitor Centre GR.123730

Terrain: Good forest track ascending gradually then a short path to the fort with two short but steep ascents.

Comments: Another walk with spectacular views throughout. Demanding in parts of the upper section.

Note: The upper area may be subject to forestry operations at certain times.

1. Starting at the door of the Visitor Centre walk round to the road, turn left, walking for 230m to a sign on the opposite side pointing to The West Highland Way.

2. Turn right here along a straight path, to a kissing gate entering the forest. Go through and ascend to a wide track with a small waymark sign again to The West Highland Way.

3. Follow this sign turning left to walk 700m to another sign at a fork in the track. Turn off to the right following the sign and ascend through the forest on The West Highland Way.

4. In the upper stages you go around two sharp bends on the track to a waymarker post with a yellow arrow pointing up a narrow path to your right and following West Highland Way signs.

5. Ascend this path to a deer fence with a stile. Go over, turning left along a line of trees on a narrow undulating path to the fort remains. The views from the summit are outstanding in all directions.

6. Retrace your steps, walking back through the forest to where your wide track joins another wide track at the lower end of the forest. Turn right here walking for 400m to a metalled road section before turning left along a narrow path leading to a kissing gate.

7. Walk through then go between the houses onto a metalled road leading down to the main road beside the Glen Nevis Restaurant. Turn left at the main road and walk for 1.1km on the footpath to the Visitor Centre.

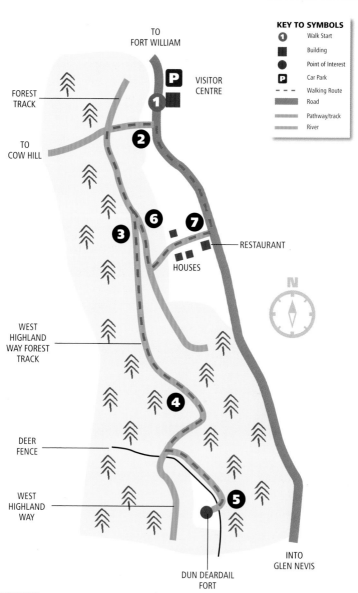

TO
FORT WILLIAM

KEY TO SYMBOLS

- Walk Start
- Building
- Point of Interest
- Car Park
- Walking Route
- Road
- Pathway/track
- River

VISITOR
CENTRE

FOREST
TRACK

TO
COW HILL

RESTAURANT

HOUSES

N

WEST
HIGHLAND
WAY FOREST
TRACK

DEER
FENCE

WEST
HIGHLAND
WAY

INTO
GLEN NEVIS

DUN DEARDAIL
FORT

NOT TO SCALE

Walk 16 - Inverlochy Castle (circular)

Start/Parking: Glen Nevis Visitor Centre GR.123730

Terrain: Majority on footpath/metalled road with 2 sections on grass/path.

Comment: An easy walk with only one slight ascent near the beginning. A picturesque and historical walk.

1. Leave the Visitor Centre by walking on a path north along by the river to a suspension bridge near the car park. Cross the bridge following the sign for 'Ben Path' and pass Achintee (B&B) on your left. The Visitor Centre is now on the opposite side of the river.

2. You come to a corner of the field where a sign points left to 'Ben Path'. Follow this, walking on a straight, ascending path for 250m to some steps over a stone wall.

3. Cross the steps then turn left on a stony farm track towards the Ben Nevis Inn and wood walking for 200m to the single track metalled road. Continue on this undulating road for 2km passing an electricity sub -station on your right, with houses on your left.

4. You come to a junction with a sign pointing back to Achintee path. Turn left here, walking a short distance to the main A82 road. Turn right now, passing the Ben Nevis Industrial Estate and walking for 1.3km to a minor road on your left leading to Inverlochy Castle. A sign is at the junction. Walk around the bend to the castle and explore this interesting ruin.

5. Turn right on the road at the side of the castle, walking down a short lane and under a railway bridge. Cross a stile on your right into a field and follow the grass path along the riverbank, crossing a wide water channel as you go towards Inverlochy.

6. On reaching the houses walk along by the village shops to some traffic lights on the A82. Turn right, walking to the small roundabout at the entrance to Glen Nevis. Turn left here, walking on the footpath for 2km back to the Visitor Centre.

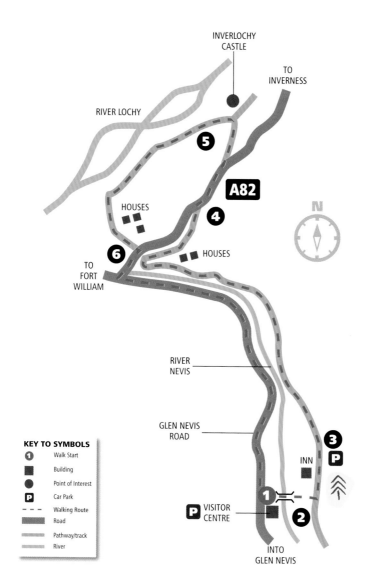

INVERLOCHY
CASTLE

TO
INVERNESS

RIVER LOCHY

5

A82

4

HOUSES

6

TO
FORT
WILLIAM

HOUSES

N

RIVER
NEVIS

GLEN NEVIS
ROAD

3
P

INN

1

P VISITOR
CENTRE

2

INTO
GLEN NEVIS

KEY TO SYMBOLS

- **1** Walk Start
- ■ Building
- ● Point of Interest
- P Car Park
- – – – Walking Route
- ▬ Road
- ▬ Pathway/track
- ▬ River

NOT TO SCALE

Start/Parking: Braveheart Car Park, north end of Glen Nevis Forest in Glen Nevis. GR.122737

Terrain: Footpath/road with a gradual ascent but mostly flat.

Comment: A good walk with refreshment at the distillery!

1. Turn left from Braveheart car park, walking on the footpath to the roundabout at the entrance to Glen Nevis.

2. At this roundabout turn right, walking on the A82 for 2km to the junction of the A830 road at Victoria Bridge and passing Ben Nevis Industrial Estate on your right.

3. Walk straight across the mini roundabout and the distillery is on your right 100m further. The distillery is open most days for visits, showing the history of whisky making in Fort William and other interesting items as well as offering refreshments.

4. Leaving the distillery, turn left retracing your steps to the last turning on your left before the Glen Nevis roundabout.

5. After passing the industrial estate again, turn left then right following the signs to Achintee path. Gradually ascend on a single-track road to a wood and the Ben Nevis Inn at Achintee.

6. Walk along the track ahead for 200m to some steps over a stone wall on your right. Go over, and then descend a straight path to the lower end beside the River Nevis.

7. Turn right to the suspension bridge ahead of you. Cross the bridge to go through the Visitor Centre car park to the main Glen Nevis road.

8. Turn right walking for 800m back to Braveheart car park at the end of the forest.

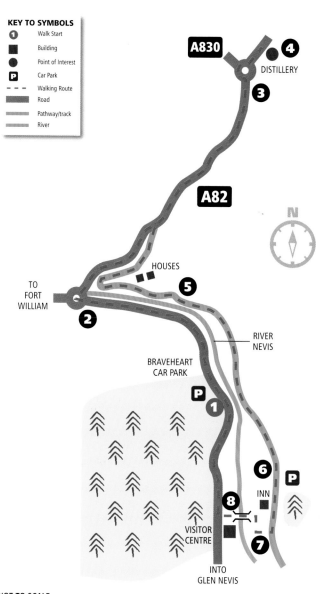

KEY TO SYMBOLS

- ① Walk Start
- ■ Building
- ● Point of Interest
- 🅿 Car Park
- - - - Walking Route
- Road
- Pathway/track
- River

A830

④ DISTILLERY

③

A82

HOUSES

⑤

TO
FORT
WILLIAM

②

RIVER
NEVIS

BRAVEHEART
CAR PARK

🅿

①

⑥

🅿

⑧

INN

VISITOR
CENTRE

⑦

INTO
GLEN NEVIS

NOT TO SCALE

Walk 18 - Loch Linnhe View Walk (circular)

Start: Roundabout at the entrance to the large supermarket near the railway station. GR.105744

Terrain: Footpath, small stone/shale and riverbank. Easy walking.

Comment: A flat enjoyable easy walk with views of mountains, Loch Linnhe, Inverlochy Castle and the canal. Well worth the effort.

1. Start at the roundabout at the entrance to the large supermarket near the railway station. Take the path/cycleway along the side of a pub and continue behind a Travel Inn, following Great Glen Way signs. Follow it between a cluster of houses and cross a bridge over the River Nevis.

2. Turn left at the far side to take you along the riverbank and round to a kissing gate at the far end. Go through then turn left. Walk for 80m on the road then cross the Soldier's Bridge over the River Lochy, following the Great Glen Way sign. Ascend the steps at the far side. Emerging on the road, cross with care. Turn left and walk on the pavement following Great Glen Way signs.

3. Follow Great Glen Way signs and continue on the road, turning left to the side of Loch Linnhe, with good views all round. Stay on this road round the outskirts of the estate then at the far end, walk along the narrow path. Keep Loch Linnhe on your left and a sports field on the right.

4. Follow the path past a waterfall and ascend through trees onto the side of the Caledonian Canal. Turn right here and walk on the towpath, keeping the canal on your left. When you arrive at the railway line, cross with care and cross the main A830 road. Ascend the side of Neptune's Staircase to view the locks.

5. After viewing, return to the main road at the swing bridge, cross and turn left, walking to a mini roundabout 1.7km along near the fuel station. Turn immediately right on a foot/cycle path towards a white building leading to Inverlochy Castle. Passing the castle, continue on the road for 15m to the junction.

6. Turn right at the junction of the road and follow it past the white house bearing left, and back over the small wooden bridge, turning right on your original path back through the kissing gate. Walk along the riverbank again and over a footbridge, retracing your steps through the housing estate and back to the roundabout by the supermarket where you started.

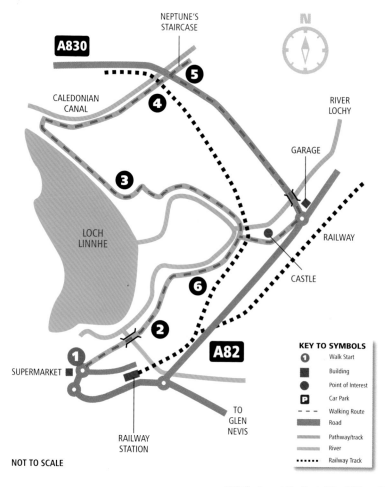

KEY TO SYMBOLS

❶	Walk Start
■	Building
●	Point of Interest
🅿	Car Park
– – –	Walking Route
	Road
	Pathway/track
	River
••••••	Railway Track

NOT TO SCALE

Start/Parking: Glen Nevis Visitor Centre GR.123730

Terrain: Footpath/stony track with a gradual ascent followed by a steep descent.

Comment: Views from the summit are exceptional, take a camera. It is recommended that you do this walk in the direction stated, as the ascent is very steep in reverse.

1. From the Visitor Centre, turn right and walk on the footpath to the roundabout at the entrance to Glen Nevis. Continue into Fort William centre, walking along the main street to the roundabout near the police station, a total of 4.4km.

2. Turn left at this roundabout and ascend Lundavra Road through the housing estate following the sign at the roundabout for Upper Auchintore. Pass houses on both sides as you walk to the cattle grid at the top of the road.

3. Past the cattle grid is a 5-bar gate on your left and a notice states 'access needed at all times'. Walk through the space at the side of the gate on a firm but stony track leading to Cow Hill mast. There are good views of Ben Nevis and surrounding area.

4. The track winds around the hillside before coming to a green post with a path leading off right. Keep left on the main track going over a stile next to a 5-bar gate then winding round to the mast ahead. Take care not to venture too far away from the mast especially in low visibility.

5. Leaving the mast, retrace your steps back to the green post now on your left that you passed earlier. Turn left onto a path, which leads to a kissing gate, before descending steeply through the forest.

6. You come to a wide track crossing your path below. There is a handrail down some steps there. Cross straight over the track to another kissing gate then along a straight path for 120m to the Glen Nevis road. Turn left, then first right back into the Visitor Centre on the opposite side.

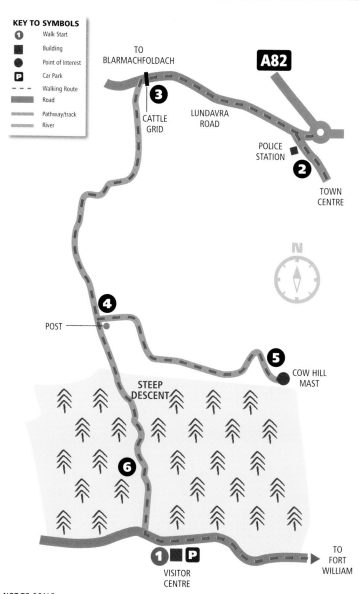

KEY TO SYMBOLS

❶	Walk Start
■	Building
●	Point of Interest
🅿	Car Park
– – –	Walking Route
	Road
	Pathway/track
	River

TO
BLARMACHFOLDACH

A82

❸

CATTLE
GRID

LUNDAVRA
ROAD

POLICE
STATION

❷

TOWN
CENTRE

N

❹

POST

❺

COW HILL
MAST

STEEP
DESCENT

❻

TO
FORT
WILLIAM

❶ ■ 🅿

VISITOR
CENTRE

NOT TO SCALE

Walk 20 - River Nevis Walk (long, circular)

Start/Parking: Glen Nevis Visitor Centre GR.123730

Terrain: Flat path easy to follow at first, becomes wet in numerous parts and more testing.

Comment: A pleasant walk by the river but can be wet towards the end of the Glen. Generally keep on the path by the river to the end of the Glen.

1. Walk to the suspension bridge at the Visitor Centre. Cross the bridge following the sign there for 'Ben path'. Continue along the riverbank passing Achintee Farm (B&B) on your left. You see the Visitor Centre on the other side.

2. At a turning left for the Ben path, carry straight on by the river. Cross four burns leading to the river before coming to a footbridge over the river near the youth hostel. Do not cross the bridge but continue along the riverbank path passing a stile on your left beside the bridge, leading up to Ben Nevis.

3. Walk around a wire fence, past another stile, cross a burn then a stile following a path to another stile at the far end of a field. This takes you back onto the main riverbank path.

4. Further on cross another stile into a large field on your left following a feint path initially beside the fence going towards a square of trees ahead. This is an ancient burial ground of the Camerons' used in the 1700's.

5. At the far side of the trees turn right to a 5-bar gate near the river, then turn left again on the path. It becomes more difficult to walk on the path as it crosses several burns before going through a wood.

6. Cross two boggy sections as the path becomes progressively harder to walk along, before ascending towards two white buildings. Walk up the steps at the side of the first building to a farm track.

7. Turn right, walking along the track, to go through two 5-bar gates at the side of a sheep pen, then through another onto the metalled road.

8. Turn right crossing two small bridges, following the road around to the right as you pass the Lower Falls car park. Cross another small bridge at Achriabhach, then turn left onto a wide track through the forest going through a 5-bar gate. Do not take the narrow path ascending the side of the forest.

9. Continue for 6km through the forest, do not deviate from this path but stay on the track until you come to a path crossing left to right.

10. Turn right here going down to a kissing gate, then walk 120m to the main Glen Nevis road. Turn left, then after a short distance turn right back to the Visitor Centre.

NOT TO SCALE

Walk 21 - Neptune's Staircase (circular)

Start/Parking: Glen Nevis Visitor Centre GR.123730

Terrain: One short ascent with most of the route on footpath.

Comment: Gain an insight into how a flight of locks work, which should be very interesting. Take care not to fall in the lock.

1. Pick up the path along by the riverbank and walk to the suspension bridge near the car park. Cross the bridge following the sign for 'Ben path'.

2. Just past the Achintee guesthouse, turn left, again following the 'Ben path' sign. Ascend the straight path to a stone wall 250m further on. Cross the steps over the wall then turn left on a trackleading to the Ben Nevis Inn and a parking area.

3. Walk along the undulating road for 2km, passing houses at the lower end. At a road junction a sign points back to Achintee path, turn left to the main A82 road. Turn right at the A82 and walk to the mini roundabout, passing the Ben Nevis Industrial Estate on your right. Take care on the busy roads.

4. At the mini roundabout, turn left onto the A830, cross the River Lochy, walking on a straight road for 1.3km to a swing bridge over the Caledonian Canal. A gate at the side of the canal leads to the flight of locks. There are 8 in total and you can watch the boats passing through on their journey to Inverness. The canal has been in use since 1822 and runs for 60 miles, passing through Loch Ness.

5. Leaving the lock area, retrace your steps to the mini roundabout, go through a gate on your right onto a walk/cyclepath taking you past a pitch and putt and a football field on your left. Just past Inverlochy Castle, turn left on a road back to the A82 road.

6. Turn right at the A82, walking to the Nevis Bridge roundabout 1.2km further on. Turn left walking on the footpath for 2km back to Glen Nevis Visitor Centre.

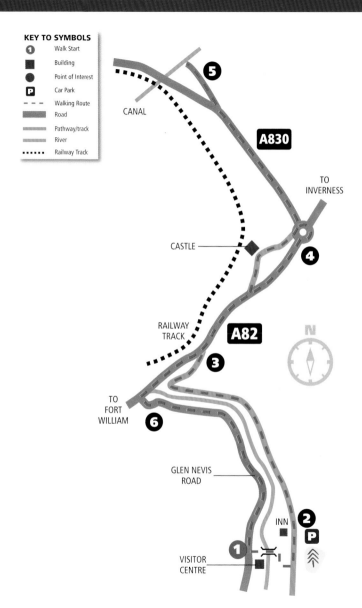

KEY TO SYMBOLS

- ❶ Walk Start
- ■ Building
- ● Point of Interest
- 🅿 Car Park
- – – – Walking Route
- ▬ Road
- ▬ Pathway/track
- ▬ River
- ••••• Railway Track

CANAL

❺

A830

TO INVERNESS

CASTLE

❹

RAILWAY TRACK

A82

❸

N

TO FORT WILLIAM

❻

GLEN NEVIS ROAD

INN

❷

🅿

❶

VISITOR CENTRE

NOT TO SCALE

Start/Parking: Glen Nevis Visitor Centre GR.123730

Terrain: Well-defined undulating track/path then a 6km walk on metalled road.

Comment: Moderately difficult with some short steep climbs.
The upper area may be subject to forestry operations at certain times.

1. Turn left from the Visitor Centre, cross the road walking to a sign 230m along the road for West Highland Way, just before the white house (B&B) on the right.

2. Turn onto a path towards the forest, go through a kissing gate, and then ascend a short path to meet a wide track. Follow the waymark sign for West Highland Way to the left.

3. You are now on a good track through the forest, 700m further on, bear right, ascending another wide track to the upper forest area.

4. There are good views of the Ben and Glen Nevis to your left. Continue for 1.7km rounding two hairpin bends in the path. Look for a waymark sign on your right at the end of the track, which points along a narrow path to your right. Continue ascending steeply for a short distance to a fence and stile.

5. Cross the stile, continue on the obvious path on The West Highland Way. Walk through a large forest for 3.2km, cross over five deer fences and pass through a firebreak in the forest.

6. Stay on this path through the second part of the forest section before crossing open grassland for 1km. Walk through a 600m section of forest before coming to a seat on your right with a signboard nearby.

7. Turn right at the signboard going off The West Highland Way, onto Caulfield's Military Road. This is initially a short section of rough track followed by a single-track metalled road.